"Grandma Margie's Tale of Redemption: Zacchaeus and Jesus"

WRITTEN BY: DR. K. T. ZULKOWSKI

ILLUSTRATED BY: INDALECIO CHAVEZ JR.

Published by Mz. Kim Productions
4263 Tierra Rejada Rd #151
Moorpark, CA 93021
www.mzkimproductions.com

ISBN: 978-1-962106-03-0

Printed in United States of America
First Printing: August 2023
Date of Copyright: July 5, 2023
Cover design by Indalecio Chavez Jr.
Illustrations by Indalecio Chavez Jr.

For permissions, please contact: Mz. Kim Productions
4263 Tierra Rejada Rd #151
Moorpark, CA 93021
www.mzkimproductions.com
mzkimproductions@gmail.com

Dedication:

To my grandmother, Margie, whose unwavering love, faith, and storytelling have shaped me into the person I am today. Your wisdom, compassion, and ability to find redemption in every story have inspired me to create this book. Thank you for teaching me the power of forgiveness and for sharing your heart with me and the world.

I also dedicate this book to all the grandparents and elders who lovingly pass down their stories and traditions to the next generation. Your guidance and wisdom are invaluable, and your presence in our lives is a precious gift.

Lastly, I dedicate this book to all the children and young readers who are on their own journey of growth and understanding. May this story remind you of the potential for change within yourselves and others, and may it inspire you to embrace empathy, compassion, and forgiveness in your own lives.

With love and gratitude,
Dr. K.T. Zulkowski

Dear Readers,

I am delighted to share with you "Grandma Margie's Tale of Redemption: Zacchaeus and Jesus." This heartwarming story holds a special place in my heart, and I hope it resonates with you and your loved ones.

Throughout my career as a filmmaker and author, I have strived to create stories that inspire, uplift, and encourage personal growth. "Grandma Margie's Tale of Redemption" embodies these values, exploring themes of forgiveness, redemption, and the power of compassion.

In this book, readers are invited to embark on a journey with Grandma Margie, Zipporah, and Zion as they learn about the transformative power of forgiveness through the story of Zacchaeus. As Grandma Margie shares this tale, she imparts valuable lessons about empathy, understanding, and the importance of second chances.

I believe that storytelling is a powerful tool for teaching important moral values and fostering personal growth. Through the pages of this book, I hope to inspire young readers to reflect on their own actions and choices, and to embrace the potential for change and growth within themselves and others.

Furthermore, "Grandma Margie's Tale of Redemption" aims to promote cultural awareness by introducing children to biblical stories and teachings in an accessible and relatable manner. It encourages respect for diverse beliefs and backgrounds, fostering an understanding of different perspectives.

I am grateful for the opportunity to share this story with you, and I hope that it brings joy, inspiration, and meaningful discussions into your homes and classrooms. May it remind us all of the power of forgiveness and the potential for transformation that lies within each of us.

With warm regards,
Dr. K.T. Zulkowski

Educational Value:

This book offers significant educational value for young readers. It introduces them to important moral values such as forgiveness, empathy, and compassion. Through the story of Zacchaeus, children learn about the power of transformation and the potential for growth and change within themselves and others.

Additionally, the book encourages critical thinking as readers reflect on the choices and actions of the characters. It prompts discussions about the consequences of our actions and the importance of making amends when we have done wrong.

Furthermore, "Grandma Margie's Tale of Redemption" promotes cultural awareness by introducing children to biblical stories and teachings in an accessible and relatable manner. It fosters an understanding of different perspectives and encourages respect for diverse beliefs and backgrounds.

Overall, this book not only entertains but also educates, making it a valuable addition to any child's library.

"Grandma Margie's Tale of Redemption: Zacchaeus and Jesus"

WRITTEN BY: DR. K. T. ZULKOWSKI

ILLUSTRATED BY: INDALECIO CHAVEZ JR.

"Gather around, my dear Zipporah and Zion. It's storytime! Today, I want to share with you a story about a man named Zacchaeus, who learned the power of forgiveness and redemption."

"Zaccheus was a tax collector, but he was not well-liked by the people. Let me share with you a scripture from Luke 19:2: 'A man was there by the name of Zaccheus; he was a chief tax collector and was wealthy.'"

"Who is Zaccheus, Grandma?"

"Zacchaeus had heard about Jesus and wanted to see Him. In Luke 19:3, it says, 'He wanted to see who Jesus was, but because he was short, he could not see over the crowd.'"

"Why is Zacchaeus tryingto see Jesus, Grandma?"

"Yes, my dear Zipporah. Jesus saw Zacchaeus and called him by name. In Luke 19:5, it says, 'Zacchaeus, come down immediately. I must stay at your house today.'"

"Jesus noticed Zacchaeus, Grandma!"

"Zacchaeus is going to meet Jesus, Grandma!"

"That's right my dear Zion. Zacchaeus was overjoyed to meet Jesus. In Luke 19:6, it says, 'So he came down at once and welcomed him gladly.'"

Jesus saw Zacchaeus and knew that deep down, he wanted to change. Jesus was drawn to him because He saw the goodness in his heart, even though others didn't.

"What did Jesus and Zacchaeus talk about, Grandma?"

"Jesus showed Zacchaeus love and acceptance. In Luke 19:9, it says, 'Jesus said to him, "Today salvation has come to this house, because this man, too, is a son of Abraham."'"

Jesus wanted to show Zacchaeus that He accepted and loved him, despite what others thought. He wanted to give Zacchaeus a chance to change and be forgiven.

"Zacchaeus changed, Grandma!"

"Yes, grand baby Zion. Zacchaeus
repented and promised to make amends.
In Luke 19:8, it says, 'But Zacchaeus stood
up and said to the Lord, "Look, Lord! Here
and now I give half of my possessions to
the poor, and if I have cheated anybody
out of anything, I will pay back four times
the amount."'"

When Zacchaeus spent time with
Jesus, he felt a deep sense of love
and forgiveness. He realized the
wrongs he had done and wanted
to make things right.

Grandma Margie,
why is Zacchaeus
saying those things?

"Now, let's turn to another scripture that teaches us about forgiveness. In Matthew 6:14, Jesus says, 'For if you forgive other people when they sin against you, your heavenly Father will also forgive you.'"

"Let's pray together, my darlings, and ask God to help us forgive others and seek forgiveness when we make mistakes."

"I'm sorry, Zion, for taking your toy without asking. Will you forgive me?"

"Of course, Zipporah. I forgive you."

"That's the spirit, my loves. Forgiveness brings healing and strengthens our relationships."

"It feels good to help others, Grandma Margie."

"Yes, my dear Zion. When we show kindness and forgiveness, we spread love and make the world a better place."

"Let's end our day with a prayer, my darlings. Dear God, thank you for teaching us about forgiveness and redemption. Help us to forgive others and seek forgiveness when we make mistakes. Amen."

"Remember, my sweethearts, forgiveness is a gift we give ourselves and others. Let's continue to spread love and forgiveness wherever we go."

"We will, Grandma Margie!"

"Thank you for teaching us about forgiveness. We love you, Grandma!"

"I love you both more than words can express. Now, let's embark on more adventures and discover the beauty of forgiveness together"

www.ingramcontent.com/pod-product-compliance
Lightning Source LLC
Chambersburg PA
CBHW041531120626
46551CB00018B/2658